Vigil

Vigil

poems by
Dudgrick Bevins

Vigil

Published by bd-studios.com in New York City, 2021
Copyright © 2021 by Dudgrick Bevins

Design by luke kurtis

ISBN 978-1-950231-96-6

This collection is a work of fiction. All characters are fictionalized. Any resemblance to those living or dead is purely coincidental.

All Rights Reserved. No part of this publication may be reproduced, stored in a retrieval system or transmitted in any form or by any means without the prior permission in writing of copyright holders and of the publisher.

Dedicated to the Ghosts and the Haunted of

The Frontier Middle School shooting,
Lake Moses, Washington,
February 2, 1996

The Bethel Reginal High School shooting,
Bethel, Alaska,
February 19, 1997

The Pearl High School shooting,
Pearl, Mississippi,
October 1, 1997

The Health High School shooting,
West Paducah, Kentucky,
December 1, 1997

Westside Middle School shooting,
Craighead, Arkansas,
March 24, 1998

The Thurston School shooting,
Springfield, Oregon,
May 21, 1998

The Columbine High School shooting,
Littleton, Colorado,
April 20, 1999

The Santana High School shooting,
Santee, California,
March 5, 2001

The John McDonogh High School shooting,
New Orleans, Louisiana
April 14, 2003

The Red Lake Senior High School shooting,
Red Lake, Minnesota,
March 21, 2005

The Chardon High School shooting,
Chardon, Ohio,
February 27, 2012

The Sandy Hook Elementary School shooting,
Newtown, Connecticut,
December 14, 2012

The Marysville Pilchuck High School shooting,
Marysville, Washington,
October 24, 2014

The Marshall Country High School shooting,
Draffenville, Kentucky,
January 23, 2018

and

The Marjory Stoneman Douglas High School shooting,
Parkland, Florida,
February 14, 2018

and the hundreds of others
who could fill a volume of their own

"This is what our dying looks like."
    —from "Another Elegy" by Jericho Brown

"This is not an anomaly. The United States is suffering from a gun-violence epidemic, one that has been spilling into schools."
    —Amanda Erickson of *The Washington Post*

"Rid of the world's injustice, and his pain,
    He rests at last beneath God's veil of blue:
    Taken from life when life and love were new
The youngest of the martyrs here is lain
Fair as Sebastian, and as early slain."
    —from "The Grave of Keats" by Oscar Wilde

"The voices sort of faded away…"
    —Samuel Granillo,
    Columbine shooting survivor

Contents

Introduction	13
Vigil I.	25
Vigil II.	28
Vigil III.	31
Vigil IV.	33
Memorial I.	34
Graves	36
Rachel Alhadeff	39
Richard Beigel	41
Isaiah Clark	44
Evan Dworet	47
Daniel Engle	49
Sean Feis	53
Kelly Guttenburg	55
Lance Hixon	58
Michael Ibsen	60
Memorial II.	62
Mark Jacobus	64

Anne-Marie Kowalski	67
Matthew Loughran	70
Kyle Montalto	72
Patrick Neily	74
Steven Oliver	76
Lisa Petty	79
Brian Quezada	81
Patti Ramsey	83
Memorial III.	86
Stephanie Schachter	88
John Turner	90
Lauren Ulman	92
Cassie Vanderbilt	94
Nicole Wang	96
Austin Xavier	99
Jennifer Yarborough	101
William Zachariah	105
Forgetting	108
After the Vigil	112
American Hymn	123
About the Author	167

Introduction

In the opening poem of *The Spoon River Anthology*, Edgar Lee Masters writes, "Where are Elmer, Herman, Bert, Tom and Charley, / The weak of will, the strong of arm, the clown, the boozer, the fighter? / All, all are sleeping on the hill." Since eleventh grade literature, I have imagined that hill, that eternal resting place overlooking the small world where the dead once conducted their lives. Masters, with humor and humanity, gives life to the dead with the gift of voice, letting them speak from their graves. In some cases, the dead say what was unspoken in life. They uncover mysteries and expose secrets, but mostly, they reveal that death is much like life — full of gossip and idle chatter. In Masters' view, death changes little. There is no great light, no great revelation; there is only the recounting of old stories.

  Douglas Coupland, following Masters' lead, expanded the idea of a beyond-the-grave narrative in his novel *Hey Nostradamus*.

Here Cheryl, the protagonist and narrator of part one, recounts the time up until she died in a fictional 1988 school shooting. When she says, "Stillness is what I have here now — wherever here is. I'm no longer a part of the world and I'm still not yet a part of what follows," I can't help but imagine her as another voice speaking from Masters' hill. Cheryl's voice, and the voices of the three other narrators that follow her, are single-minded. They focus entirely on a mass school shooting and the ripples it left in the minds of the dead as well as the living. While Masters addresses every corpse buried in the cemetery, Coupland focuses on one and how that one impacted the lives of others.

Vigil, in a way, is my ode to those two authors. From Masters, I take my form and my location: both take place in a graveyard on the hill — and this hill, I imagine as the city cemetery in my hometown. As a teenager, I sat on the hill, surrounded by tombstones, and looked over my little slice of the south. I could see the whole of Main Street, the elementary school, the courthouse, the business district of Ellijay, Georgia. My friend Hannah was usually with me. Through some psychic connection, or human instinct, or adolescent wishful thinking, I felt we were thinking the same thoughts.

What were the lives like of the people whose company we were keeping? And what about the lives of those who sometimes visited the graves? Impossible questions that tug at the heart, that demand answers despite being unanswerable, questions that elicit only speculation. *Vigil* is my speculation.

From both Masters and Coupland, I attempt to borrow the humanity that each author gives to their dead. Cheryl is not perfect. She has her secrets and her pain; she wants to know and be known; she wants to speak and makes us want to listen. Likewise, Masters gives his chorus of ghostly voices significant imperfections — they are flawed characters. They lie. They manipulate. They tell the story that best fits the narratives they have of themselves, creating a Rashomon effect for the reader. I hope that in some small way, I am giving my characters the dignity of imperfection, and enough pride to be complicated, flawed, and compelling.

But a school shooting is a touchy subject, especially with the way Americans fetishize youth, guns, and death. Despite phrases like "he's a terror," "the terrible two's," and "my little monster," children are relegated to the realm of purity and innocence. Any suggestion that a child might not be an angel underneath is unspeakable.

If this were not the case, every school would have prophylactic centered sex education to prevent the spread of children. In much the same way we see the youth as symbols of hope and aspiration that must have their innocence protected at all costs, we revere the dead as saints. No one says at a funeral, "yeah, he sure was an asshole." And this is not just for the sake of propriety. In my own experience, I have seen the mistakes and shortcomings of the dead erased, covered over with a gloss of imagined perfection. To combine the two — dead children — is dangerous, but to then speak ill (or worse, truthfully) of these tiny saints, well, that is un*speak*able. But it is the flaws that make them human. To present young people as anything other than developing, flawed, lost, and mixed up is dishonest and disrespectful. Still, I would say the same thing of any adult character I wrote into being. Luckily, I based none of the ghosts who speak here on real people. Each is from my imagination entirely.

While it's true that this is a fictional work, the emotions it contains come from my life. I came of age in a time of institutional collapse. My first memories of the news are of the Rodney King riots, the Waco siege, and the John and Lorena Bobbitt case. Nothing seemed stable: not the police, not the public, not even marriage, or the body. Then once these events cycled out of the news, along came the Unabomber, the Oklahoma City bombing, and the Centennial Olympic bombing in Atlanta, just an hour away from my hometown. Timothy McVeigh, Ted Kazcynski, and Eric Rudolf made it impossible to view any place — government building, healthcare facility, recreational facility — as entirely safe. Then on April 20, 1999, when I was near the end of my seventh-grade year, the Columbine massacre happened, and school was no longer safe.

Like the security theater of post-9/11 airports, my school took the least effective but most visible actions possible: it outlawed fingernail clippers, encouraged students to buy clear plastic book bags, banned fake bullet casing belts, and cracked down on "offensive" t-shirts. All of this was for show and did nothing to stop the bomb threat that came on the last day of school that year. Fortunately, there was no explosion, just the looming threat that anyone, anywhere, at any time, could decide to end your life.

On the anniversary of the Columbine massacre, some of my high school friends wore signs pinned to their shirts that said, "I know why they did it." The statement was both profound and insensitive — two reasons why they didn't get away with it very long. For me, it was thought-provoking. I, too, knew the feeling of isolation and difference that school breeds for kids that are even remotely queer.

There was Jamie who pushed me in the hall every day and called me gay. There was Tasha, who made fun of my hair, clothes, and pimples; she asked me, "Why do you dress so ugly?" Even Mrs. Burnette pulled me into the hall and questioned me with her tiny southern voice, "Dudgrick, why do you want to dress so ugly? Do you need to paint your nails and have that hair?" She was talking about my band t-shirts, baggy pants, earrings, combed over mohawk, and blue-glitter nails. However well-intended and genuine her concern may have been, it only made me feel that much more isolated. My small acts of individualism and rebellion elicited ostracization. There was a clear divide between who and what was acceptable and who and what wasn't. In the "wasn't" group, members could easily imagine why "they did it."

Admitting to understanding why they did it is dangerous because many people conflate understanding with approval. But these two verbs are not equal. When I heard about the bullying of Eric Harris and Daniel Klebolt, I sympathized. I understood their feelings. I knew how someone could feel like their bullies, and the system that supported them, deserved to suffer in the same way. *Vigil* expresses those feelings — another blasphemy never to be spoken aloud! But let me be clear, I never supported their actions, nor do the characters within, nor did my friends with the signs. Instead, knowing why they did it is about seeing, at least in part, systemic problems. These problems range from the trauma of young people and the perpetual neglect of the adults in their lives to all-too-easy access to weapons and bomb-making materials. Not to mention a society that encourages boys (who make up almost one hundred percent of school shooters) to externalize their feelings as anger.

    These problems became more apparent to me once I transitioned from being the weird high school student to the odd high school teacher. I carried with me the baggage of adolescent awkwardness, of difference, of feeling othered. I wanted to ensure that none of my students ever felt what Eric and Daniel felt. I wanted to ensure that even if they thought what I felt, that they had positive outlets for those emotions — not just anger externalized as violence. This desire to help young people was the impetus for starting a creative writing class at the school where I work. I wanted to make a safe space for all to express themselves, to give voice to the otherwise unspoken thoughts and feelings floating through the hallways, at lunch, or in calculus.

    I felt good about my work in creative writing and still do. However, on February 14, 2018, the Parkland, Florida shooting occurred. This tragedy made real, for the first time since I had become a full-time teacher in 2014, the fact that these supposedly safe spaces were vulnerable and permeable. Schools were not a shield, but at best a net, letting through the small seemingly nonthreatening fish. I was reliving my Columbine feelings all over again but from the perspective of the teacher. Parkland has strong academics and clubs that encourage expression; according to some reports, creative expression was an expectation. At the very least, Parkland provides an overwhelming array of opportunities for that expression: drama, speech and debate, chorus, thespians' club, newspaper, step, and spoken word, to name a few. Yet, despite the vast array of options, Nikolas Cruz still brought a shotgun to school. He killed seventeen people and injured seventeen more, thus surpassing Columbine as the deadliest school shooting in American history. To say I was afraid is not accurate; I feel like I know my students and trust them — I don't see violence in their eyes or hearts, nor do I hear it in their words. But I imagine this was it-could-never-happen-to-me thinking, the same kind of thinking shared by the teachers at the all-too-many schools that have suffered from gun violence.

I couldn't help but wonder how the surviving teachers felt about the shooting, about their deceased students, and about the circus that follows any great travesty — especially one involving children. Taking that as my point of departure, I began this book. I know I'm not the first to attempt to capture the experience of a school shooting. *American Horror Story: Murder House* did so eloquently with the library shooting scene. Gus Van Sant's *Elephant* is another striking example. However, both of these works focus on shooters. I did not want to give voice to the killers: Their heinous acts spoke for themselves. There is nothing left to say that isn't a plea for sympathy. No, like Masters and Coupland, I wanted to hear from the dead; I wanted the story told in their voices from their graves.

Furthermore, as a student when the Columbine massacre occurred and a teacher when the Parkland massacre occurred, I had my ghosts to exorcise. That is, the looming specter of these events and the mild but consistent survivor's guilt I felt. From there, the teacher's voice was born.

Sue Klebolt, mother of Daniel Klebolt, one of the two Columbine shooters, said:

> There's no way to quantify the psychological damage of those who were in the school, or who took part in rescue or cleanup efforts. There's no way to assess the magnitude of a tragedy like Columbine, especially when it can be a blueprint for other shooters who go on to commit atrocities of their own. Columbine was a tidal wave.

What follows are the splashes on the shoreline of life after one of these tragedies. It is the account of twenty-six students and one teacher trying to reconcile the irreconcilable. It is an account that can only be told through fiction, as the dead cease to speak for themselves. It is a kind of looking, looking down from Masters' hill, as well as looking down from the cemetery hill where I sat with Hannah. It is my hope, too, that it will provide an opportunity for listening, listening to the sadder, darker parts of the American hymn. I hope that if you listen carefully, you can hear America singing, singing a mourning song, a dirge.

— DB, April 20, 2019

Vigil

Vigil I.

Flowers woven
between twisted
wires on a chain
link
fence surrounding
the football stadium.

A
makeshift memorial
on this, the night,
of the vigil.

Names written in floral wreaths
and colors:

    red
    and
    white
    and
    lily
    and
    rose —

poems and photos,
teddy bears,
a pair of shoes:
pieces of a puzzle

never
meant
to be
assembled.

Inside:
the harsh blue tint of flood
lights,
bleachers filled with
candlelit faces;
hands holding
little lights
and singing
as if it were Christmas,
only these songs
are from a hymnal
of mourning.

Vigil II.

    Tears
    and
    prayers:

both for currency
and communication —
wet fingers wipe
tired eyes and red
cheeks get stained by

    mascara
    running.

Bleachers as cold as gunmetal
never pressed against a forehead
press now against legs
in offseason weather —
these lights are not for Friday nights.

The sky, grey; nothing
no one knows
is worth saying now,
but voices still keep spraying

    words
    words
    words —

as if they can speak reality
into a different
form of being,
or maybe raise
the
dead.

Someone's pastor says,
"let us
bow our
heads
and think of the
life, eternal,
God had given
his children,
and take comfort
in knowing
they will never have to live
the suffering of men.
They were taken early —

saved
from
sin."

Vigil III.

Someone
    looks in
    through cracks
    in the wall
    of the funerary
    wreaths.

Someone
    looks out
    from the stadium,
    past the memorial,
    past the lights,
    into the parking lot,
    lost.

Someone
    weeps for the dead,
    and weeps for their hate,
    and weeps
    for the sake of weeping.

Someone
    thinks "it could have been me"
    and cries because
    she is relieved.

Vigil IV.

This
world
is
a
fractured
        place.

Memorial I.

Later
something more
    permanent
    (than
    death)
    erected
with the names of the fallen —
four walls:
a black cube
of granite
on the front lawn
of the school;
and there,
names
engraved
along with dates
for birth and death —
    the latter,
    a day
    that everyone listed shares.

It's one thing more than many of them ever
 shared before.

What a shame.

What a pity.

None of them lived
to see
their friends
bonding
in misery.

Graves

The parents agreed,
that in a show of solidarity,
they would bury all the children
in rows, alphabetically
as if they were seated for
picture day
or the graduation they
would never see.

They said
they wanted
for all of them to be visited
when one of them was visited;

and, so it was.

And from the city cemetery
anyone could easily see
>>the town
>>the school
>>and the stadium seats;
>>it overlooked all
>>the way many believed God
>>was looking after their dead
>>babies.

And maybe he was,
or maybe
those babies
were unsettled,
couldn't rest,
not with all the life
they had left.

So on the hill they talked,
and they laughed,
telling the stories of
and before death.

Rachel Alhadeff

I am singing to you
from the grave.

Soprano section,
up here on the hill,
leader of the
cemetery choir.

        Listen: a song!

I heard the first shots fired
I heard the first screams loosed
I heard the first stampede coming

        towards
        my classroom.

        A drumming of feet.

        A chorus of fear.

Their voices were singing,
rising and falling,
in the harsh acoustics of
cinder block walls.

        But it was
        our door
        they entered: calmly
        coolly,
        guns
        hanging
        at their sides
        like the voices rising.

Eyes shut tightly —
then the firing.

Richard Beigel

Walt Whitman
      sang America,
      contemplating a blade
      of grass.
      He saw the whole country —
      every man and woman
      dwelling there —
      in the green
      of growth.
      He saw it quiver in the wind.

But I watched
    the draining of blood.
    Mine and the boy
    beside me; each stream
    running to meet the
    other.
    Red and red reaching
    across the dirty tile floor.
    I wonder what Whitman
    would have seen there.

The blood of boy
> against boy,
> of boy against country,
> a Civil War of sorts.
> What would he have seen
> in the reflections of their gun,
> so clean
> so polished
> so bright.
>
> What song would he have sung?

Isaiah Clark

We were in the middle of production,
three shows left:
Friday,
Saturday,
and the Sunday matinée.

    Mrs. Miller was still tweaking our work.

Rehearsals didn't end.

    She had us running laps and lines,
    but I didn't mind
    because I had the lead:
    "Nobody"
    in *Do Not Go Gentle.*

A homeless boy
squatting in a house
with an impending estate sale
about to kick him out…
and with only a ghost
and flashbacks to
keep him company.

    Can a ghost say
    with a straight face,
    "it still haunts me?"

I got the part
because I was
small and thin,
but I didn't mind
because I was in.

> Plus, I knew there'd be no part
> for me in Richard Lortz *Voices*,
> where between the husband
> and the wife I'd be too petite
> to have a role, so I enjoyed
> what I could.

Let's say,
even if I had known
I wouldn't have stayed
home
because in death
I got my next biggest role
as top billing in the vigil.

> But for this role
> I still wonder
> why they chose
> me.

Evan Dworet

    I
could have stopped it.

It would have been as easy
as speaking,
as coughing up words,
as saying:

    I
see them coming
with their boots and guns.

    I
could have been Paul Revere.

    I
could have shouted:

        RUN!

But no one wants to be the first to speak.

No one wants to be the snitch.

No one,
not even me,
wants to be
a tattletale,
so, I was silent then —

>	a ghost in the hallways
>	not saying
>	what could have saved
>
>	our lives.

Daniel Engle

Rachel will tell you
she was the first to go,
but she is wrong,
you know.

She likes the title
and the drama,
      "first victim,"
        and rightfully so,
        who wouldn't?

She keeps the gore low,
      sticks to the storytelling,
      and she tells a good story,
      uses those similes and metaphors,
      that shit we learned in school.

But
the
truth is messier: bloodier.

They entered the south door,
everyone laughing at the clothes they wore.

    See, they came in
    with camo and headbands,
    guns and knives hanging
    from their waistbands.

We were looking
for orange toy caps
cause no one believed
that crap
could happen
here,
like that.

But
they
pulled
out
those guns
and fired —

        at nothing first…

        maybe just to scare us.

But then they aimed as we ran for the stairs.

    Bang — they shot Sean.

    Bang — Lance was next.

    Then Michael.

    Then Mark.

We lay there bleeding,
    Lance pleading,
    everyone crying
    for their life.

One stood over me,
pressed his gun to my
temple and said,

    "you don't even know my
    name. It's Derrick, by the way."

Sean Feis

    I wish
    they had
    buried me
    in
    my letterman's jacket.

I wish
my mother
had put
my
cleats in my coffin.

    I wish
    they hadn't
    shot me
    in my face.

I would
have liked an open
casket for my family.

    A face for my mother
    to kiss me goodbye,
    more than a mound of teeth
    and flesh, but a face.

A face to catch the tears
I know they must have cried.

Kelly Guttenburg

Death
is supposed to be
eternal rest

> but
> I still feel
> as tired
> as I ever did.

The teachers thought I didn't care,
said my posture —

> head down
> or arms in my sweater —

communicated indifference
and attitude;

    but I was
    just so tired
    I couldn't even
    pretend to really
    be there.

But,
when I was lying there bleeding
I didn't feel hurt, only
a kind of sleepiness,

like I would finally rest,

like there would be silence,

like my parents wouldn't be fighting,

like, maybe, I could sleep forever.

But it turns out,
this hill is nothing but chatter,
talking and
talking about

      nothing.

      It's like I never left class.

I wish I could pull myself
inside my sweater
and put my head down forever.

Lance Hixon

It's surprising
how much the body
wants to live.

It fights.

It resists.

Like the hole he shot in my chest,
all wounds want to heal over
and the body
just keeps working.

There is a gurgle of blood.

> I don't question it; I've
> seen enough movies
> to know that it's normal.

But I just kept thinking:

> I'll live.
> I'll live.

I just kept thinking:

> My blood will clot.
> My body will heal.

I just kept thinking:

> Don't die.
> Not here.

Michael Ibsen

The living talk
like the dead don't hear,
like just because we rot
we've lost our ears.

> But
> Earth
> is never
> far away;
> never
> out of
> earshot.

Always close enough that I can hear them say:

> "what a good boy he was,"
> "what a kind young man,"
> "what a dear little angel,"
> how proud they are that I am theirs.

It hurts because they're wrong:

>because they remember only
what they want,
because they ignore what
doesn't seem to fit.

No one ever says,

>maybe he was mean,
maybe he deserved it.

Memorial II.

A mother

        runs her fingers
        in the grooves of
        her child's name.

Dust has gathered there,

        dust that rain
        could not remove.

She has trampled through the flowers to touch it,

        but no one has anything to say;
        they just look
        away
        from this private
        moment in a public
        space.

She weeps and wonders

      what will never be said,
      now that these
      twenty-six
      children are dead.

Mark Jacobus

They were
gunning for the
jocks and the cheer
girls
the popular kids —
the ones they wished
they could
be, but knew they never
would become.

They were gunning
for kids like me.

But would that gun
have come across my chest
if they knew
I, too,
were just pretending —
posing
as
something
I never
would be:
a straight boy,
with a girl he fucked,
and a sport he loved.

He wouldn't have aimed if he knew how similar
we were
and how
scared
we both
must
have been.

He wouldn't have aimed.

He would have called me his friend.

Anne-Marie Kowalski

The cocky jocks,
the pretty girls,
the popular kids
from yearbook
and choir,
the ones who had a table
just to themselves
at lunch:
reserved; they will tell you

        Derrick wanted them.

They
think
they're
special,
even now
with all of us,
our voices
floating in the ether,
equal
in death
where
we weren't
in school.

    He aimed at anyone he saw.

There was no particular target,
just bodies
waiting to be
corpses,
regardless of our
segregated
tables

        at lunch.

Matthew Loughran

If you see my mother,
        tell her I'm sorry,
        tell her I love her,
        tell her I miss her.

If you see my mother,
        tell her I'm not sure
        why any of this happened,
        that I never hurt
        them,
        I never
        wronged them.

If you see my mother,
> tell her Dylan wasn't my friend
> but I was kind to him;
> tell her that Derrick
> was my lab partner,
> that we joked
> and he smiled
> making fun
> of Mr. Montgomery's hair.

If you see my mother
> tell her I felt nothing;
> tell her I didn't see him coming,
> tell her he asked me no questions.

If you see my mother
> tell her I still believe
> in God.

Kyle Montalto

    I
could have stopped it,
not that day,
but

    I
could have stopped it, still.

    I
could have stopped it
when I saw them pushed around,
pushed down,
slammed against a locker,
called faggot
queer freak.

    I
could have stopped it
when Sean pushed Derrick
into the bathroom,
held him against the wall,
forearm to throat,
told him his trench coat stunk,
that his nail polish made him gay,
that he would never get laid.

    I
could have stopped it then,
said something
rather than
stand quiet
while I took my piss.

    I
had more power
than I ever realized.

Patrick Neily

I never really

    saw them.

I didn't know their names.

    Why
    should
    I
    be
    punished
    if
    I
    didn't
    even
    know
    their
    faces?

We were strangers.

>How
>could
>they
>hate,
>how
>could
>they
>take
>aim
>at
>me

>when I didn't even know their names.

Steven Oliver

If you are looking for someone
      to blame,
      blame me.

I know what I did, and
      I own that;
      I'll say it:
      I pushed them,
      I called them names.

Derrick, I called faggot;
Dylan, I called freak.

But it wasn't just me,
and it wasn't just Sean.

It
was
everyone
who
saw
but
didn't
speak.

You know,
people think jocks learn nothing in class,
that we coast by
on our coaches ask,
but one thing now sticks out:
ninth grade vocabulary,
the word "complicit."

If you are looking for someone to blame,
blame the people who didn't speak out,
the people who didn't see,
the people who made them invisible.

Lisa Petty

>I
>will
>be forever
>famous.

My name en-
graved on plaques and monuments.
My photo in the yearbook spread,
and bleeding head in the VHS
tape that leaked to the news.

>I'm
>the
>only
>girl
>ever
>to record her own murder!

I'm
the
only
girl
ever
to make a snuff film in class.

I never expected video lab to end like this!
With me
the budding star.

How glorious,
my face splayed on the TV,
and broadcast
'round the world!

Brian Quezada

They killed us both: the artsy
    queer
    queen
    from drama
    and his secret football
    lover.

They had no method, just a plan.

So, I hope you are not here looking for a reason;
    we don't keep reasons up here
    on this hill — no,
    just bodies in graves.

And stories waiting to be told, like
    how the first time
    I kissed Mark —
    it was cliché
    high school magic
    and fireworks.

Electricity.

Jolts of love and
bolts of power
coursing through me.

He said he felt the same way.

And you know,
    I would have lived
    if I hadn't stood there dumb
    looking down at his body
    in the stairwell;
    we had promised never to speak at school,
    but I could never help myself,
    or keep myself
    from watching him.

Patti Ramsey

      God
      works

in
mysterious
ways.

Who
am
I

to
question
the great
decision
maker —

      God.

Maybe those boys were his
angels
and their guns boomed in
the voice

of his glory,
welcoming us
to heaven
as early guests.

I am waiting now for my ticket
for entrance, my invitation to
be in awe of the greatness

      of God.

To stand at the side

      of God.

For my eyes to bear witness to the royal flames

    of God.

    They
    were
    for us
    a burning
    bush.

    A message
    to build
    an
    ark.

Memorial III.

Sometimes,
it's easier, she thinks,
to visit
the memorial
than the graves.

She no longer has to search
for her child's name.

She finds it instantly,
then traces each letter
imagining how he died.

She could have seen
the security tapes
but she refused
not knowing
that her imagination
was worse
than the
truth.

Stephanie Schachter

We are all waiting
on God
upon this hill.

Waiting for him
to raise the dead
and take us
to heaven.

But
there is only
silence here;
silence punctuated by that
murmur of idle chatter — the
whispers of ghosts.

No horn
is calling.

There is only
us and the hill —
our bodies entombed
in echo chambers…
no one bothers
to listen.

Are
you
listening?

John Turner

Duck
lipped
Lisa.

> I hate that bitch.
> Even now,
> thinking she's the most famous
> mound
> of dirt
> on this goddamn hill.

All they wanted,
Dylan and Derrick,
was a stage,
a platform,
a screen,

> and she
> gave them that.

She means nothing!

    Posing in the library,
    with her iZone camera
    and giving away those Polaroids
    like headshots.

I think if anyone deserved a
headshot,
it was her.

Lauren Ulman

The complaints of ghost
grow old;
it's always the same
old same old.

Like how John really
loves Lisa.

Like how Patti is so proud
to love God.

Like how Matthew
misses his mom.

Like how Sean is still
going on
about his letterman's
jacket
and ignoring what he
did to Dylan
and Derrick — how he made
them sweat and suffer.

The same stories
grow tiring,
like sitting in the same
class forever,
with the same kids
always raising their hands.

Cassie Vanderbilt

Ask Patti what she believes
      and she will tell you
      "God,
      his word,
      and that he speaks."

But when Dylan held the gun
      up to her face
      and asked
      "do you still believe?"

      She said "no"
      and "please
      don't kill me."

Funny how faith can waver
and how for others it is more stable,
like when they asked me,
hiding beneath a table
in the library,
I said yes.

But still I'm here
on this goddamned hill,
looking over the place
where I was killed.

Nicole Wang

Stop
looking
for a reason.

It wasn't because they were bullied.

It wasn't their music or games.

It wasn't the name-calling.

It wasn't the nail polish and trench coats.

It wasn't that they didn't have a table at lunch.

It was because
> they wanted to,
> and could,
> because the gun cabinet
> was unlocked
> and they had a thought
> that went unchecked.

It was because
> no one cared
> until they killed,
> because that was the only way left
> to feel real,
> to be seen,
> to heal.

It was because
> they knew
> if they wanted people to hear
> they had to fire a shot and
> let it ring in our ears.

Austin Xavier

Unpopular opinion:
I don't blame them.

    I mean,
    I've had the same thoughts,
    dreamed my path through the school,
    thought about
    where I'd plant my bombs,
    who I would
    shoot, and what
    I would say.

I've thought about it all:

    Patti's hypocrisy,
    Brian's flamboyance,
    Rachel and Richard, know-it-alls,
    And then the dumb jocks.

       I mean,
if my father had a gun
        and the cabinet unlocked
        this hill would still be full
        of teenage rot.

But I wouldn't have eaten the bullets
like Dylan and Derrick —

        no,
        I would
        have walked out
        tall and proud
        and let the police
        take me down.

Jennifer Yarborough

Laura and I were ready
to go.

We wanted out of that place and
               and we were set
                  with our college
acceptances.

       Two tickets straight to Georgia State!

We were going to be in the city
       where the real lesbians go —
       real gay bars,
       real drag shows,
       we were even trying
       to swing being roommates!

Imagine:

college freshmen,
    live-in high
    school lovers.

        It would have been a dream!

She was going to shave her head
but not her legs
or armpits;

I was ready for real
intellectualism,
not just the waxing of Richard in class,
but radical dykes ready to fight.

        It would have been a dream!

I suppose I should be happy to have Laura
up here with me on this damned hill with me…

> but we both know
> we will never get back
> the opportunity
> to stop being kids
> to change the world,
> to fight and protest.
>
> We will never get back
> that chance at freedom,
> to spread our legs
> and fly for one another,
> to be
> the big
> dykes
> on campus.

We will never hold protest signs:
we will never get to say
"end gun violence,"
or "stomp out homophobia,"
or "keep your laws off my body."

        It would have been a dream!

See, protests do no good
      when you are dead,
      but then again,
      neither does gossip
      and that hasn't stopped anyone here.

        Now it is only a dream.

William Zachariah

From the hill
you could see everything:
the stadium lights,
the flowered wall,
the parking lot
filled with cars,
people in the stands —
a sea of faces
all crying for us all.

    It's was flattering,
    really.

And we hadn't even been buried,
but somehow we
knew to gather
there, in the city
cemetery where
we used to go on
Friday nights
to neck and kiss,
or drink after the
football games…
the cops knew
to leave us be: we
were just teens
being teens.

But when we gathered
we were silent then —
still fresh in our deaths,
bullets and blood still staining
our chests —
we had nothing
yet to say.

The dead are in awe of their graves.

Forgetting

It takes five years,
        exactly,
        to stop
        the
        moments
        of silence
        held
        on the
        anniversary
        of the deaths.

                Of the murders.

                Of the end.

It takes five years,
> exactly,
> to forget,
> for one mass
> shooting to be
> replaced by another.

It takes five years,
> exactly,
> for the memorials
> of silent standing
> to become trite,
> for those who watched
> the stand off on TV
> to give up,
> to put down the torch.

It takes five years,
        exactly,
        for there to be
        too many moments to
        hold each one in silence,
        to remember with solemn stares
        the darkness of one day.

It takes five years,
        exactly,
        for the calendar to fill
        with memorial
        days, with moments
        of death counted
        in bullet casings.

It takes five years,
        exactly,
        to get a new crop
        of kids in the school,
        to forget the blood stains
        and the body chalk;
        it takes five years,
        for everyone to graduate,
        for the library and lunch room
        to be rebuilt with little plaques
        that no one reads.

It takes five years,
        exactly.

After the Vigil

    I.

The vigil
must always
            end.

II.

It takes five years,
        exactly,
        to forget,
        but only one day
        for the vigilant
        to snuff their candles,
        never to be relit.

And then the news crews return
        and shoot
        the ghosts of candles past,
        the spent bits of wax
        on paper plates,
        as cars pass by —
        seen only by their
        spinning tires —
        while an anchor's

    voice-over tells the story
    of the crowd
    from last night:
    "Hundreds gathered here,
    at the local high school
    football field,
    to mourn the fallen
    children and their peers."

And then a man comes
    with a bucket and a broom
    to clean up the proof
    of how the community cared
    with teddy bears,
    and seven-day candles,
    and wreaths and flowers…
    and with his gloved hands
    he undoes the work
    of so many mourners —

petal by petal
unfolding the silk flowers
wrapped between
the chain-link fencing.
But this is only after
he has picked up the plates,
heaped the stuffed animals
into a bag —
he surely takes one home,
gives it to his daughter
or his niece,
a little gift she'll never know
was bought with blood.

And then the classes start again:
> history and math
> resume to track
> instances along a line,
> while survivors plot
> the points of how
> they ended up alive.
> Likewise,
> there is little comfort
> in literature and science:
> beautiful words
> do nothing
> when your ears are plugged
> with the sound of gunfire.
> And what is physics
> if not the clinical language
> of how we die?

III.

>Tears
>and
>prayers:

Both dry up and
both run out —
it is the order of things,
the nature of people
to slowly snap out
of their mourning,
of their shock and surprise;
it is the order of things
for people to blow their noses

>and dry
>their eyes.

Slowly,
bleachers as cold as gunmetal
warm against the backs of calves,
and the lunchroom resumes
its usual level of gossip and attitude.
Even the library returns
in a state of full bloom:
lovers hiding among the stacks,
kissing in the invisible
nooks and cracks.

>The
>life
>they
>had
>is
>coming
>back.

Somewhere,
Someone's pastor says:
"Halleluiah,
these children
are beginning
to live again."

IV.

All those flowers unwound
from their homes in the fence,
the wreaths thrown away,
the candles dampened,
deadened, and then ditched.

The makeshift
memorial, gone,
on this,
the day after the ceremony.

The pictures,
the signs,
the names
written
in remembrance,
all,

all are forgotten now —
replaced with monolithic
granite engraved
nameplates.

One
headstone
for
all the
dead.

V.

Someone,
somewhere
                is
                remembering.

American Hymn

I.

The dead cannot speak for themselves.

Nor can we speak for them.

They are hushed — finger to their lips.

Quieted: babies put down for sleep.

But sometimes, I think I can hear them,
I think I can hear what they would whisper
if whispers were allowed inside their graves.

I keep vigil over the mounds of soil
heaped atop their bodies to
keep them warm.

And I wait.

And I remember.

And I listen.

II.

Rachel, singing!
The whole world singing!
The varied carols of grief!

Her soft soprano rattling the headstone —
put your hand here,
feel it —
wonder with me who she could have been.

And Richard!
Poet-souled corpse!
What words we will never read!
What words you will never write!
You will be remembered
through the shot of a gun.

Isaiah!
You will never leave rehearsals now!
All those memorized lines,
for nothing!
I imagine you —
great director! —
and the show you would put on
with this hill as your stage!

I see something Shakespeare!
Rachel the nun,
Richard the bard,
and Evan as the lead?

No. He's too shy to speak.

But maybe Daniel…
he could memorize
and deliver with precise annunciation —
but his acting would be cold.
A report of the facts.
Desdemona lying dead,
and all he would say
is "that's that."

Would you cast the jocks?
Sean and Lance and Michael and Mark?
Maybe, if there is a heaven,
they play football there.
Football forever — all day long —
and lacrosse on the weekends.

III.

No one ever asks which kids deserved it.

IV.

William,
forgive me for sitting atop your tombstone
but you have the best view.
It never occurred to me,
until I sat here with you,
to look for the school,
but there it is:

The building where you all ran screaming.
The football field where
flowers wove between fence links.
The bleachers where they cried.
The parking lot they carried you through
after you died.

William,
   seer of beauty in everything,
   I wonder what beauty you saw that day.
   What did you take with you?
   Can you share it with me today?

V.

Jennifer,
you fighter!
Little warrior of the school.

I'm so proud that I got to know you.

So proud that I got to teach you.

The grooves on your gravestone
are not as soft as your hair,
but they are as deep as the lines in your face
when you start to glare.

When I reach Lauren
I'll tell her you love her.
I'll tell her the two of you
are radicals,
changing the world
from your vaults of doom.

I wish I could tell you
in words you could hear,
tell your ears
and look in your eyes…

I'd say:

I saw you two,
once,
in the stairwell at lunch,
hiding
holding hands,
and then
a quick kiss.

Your love of Lauren,
dear Jennifer,
made palpable
in this secret alcove
of romance.

Yours was the gift
of student to teacher.

A reminder of what love can be.

VI.

Kelly,
I should start with an apology.
Maybe I should write you a letter
and burn it — a
gift for the gods to read,
like ashes scattered —
but you are buried.

Kelly,
I'm sorry.
I saw the marks on your arms
and I saw how you tried to hide them
with your oversized sweater's
black floppy sleeves.

Kelly,
I'm sorry.
You were hurting and I
said nothing,
and now you'll never
get to tell your story.
You'll never get
to heal the wound of silence.

And Anne-Marie,
I think I owe you too
an apology.

I saw you like
I saw others, you
alone at your lunch table,
save for the company of Kelly,
with whom you sat in solitary silence,
looking at your fingernails
and waiting for the day to end.

You were always lost in thought,
lost in thoughts I wished you'd share.
I should have pushed you more in class
to be brave,
to be bold,
to be brash.

I should have asked you,
"What are you thinking?
Where is your head at?"

VII.

Cassie,
Nicole, and
Austin:

I never got to know you and now I never will.

The distance you kept,
so carefully, kept
everyone who could have cared
at bay.

Each of you hiding,
like Kelly,
in a metaphorical hoodie
to keep your scars covered
and a smile on your face.

Cassie,
you hid so much so well,
but spite betrayed your eyes.
I could see a glimmer of hate
sparkle when hypocrisy
challenged truth.

Nicole,
I only ever saw you come to life
in class debate.
Oh, how you loved to find the flaws
of other thinkers.
But every time you'd get excited
you'd also give in,
throw up your hands
and say, "what's the point?
We can never know
what the author meant!"

And Austin,
you enigmatic loner,
a teacher should never say this,
but had I picked the shooter,
I would have chosen you.
I know it is unfair,
but your trench coat,
your dyed black greasy hair,
the hate you wore on your face,
the malice mixed with confidence
you projected as you walked
down the hallways —
all of this a cliché,
but nonetheless,
with all your silence,
what else could I assume?

I'm sorry Austin,
sorry that I didn't get to know you,
sorry I held this image in my head
when I could have said "hello"
or "how are you" instead.

VIII.

Matthew,
you were the kindest of them all…
I saw you speaking to
Derrick and Dylan,
friendly and smiling.
I saw you edit their papers
and compare class notes.
You may not have known it
but you were their friend.

Matthew,
Listen to me:
they were not aiming for you,
they were aiming for anyone.
Hate and hurt were their targets,
that's why they turned the guns
on themselves.

IX.

It is exhausting, talking to the dead.

I take a break to remember that I'm still alive.

I notice my feet sink into the soil, but only barely.

None of you have been buried long enough.

The mounds of dirt still look fresh: no grass just yet.

I smell the mulchy smell of overturned topsoil.

It mixes with the cool dampness of the clay.

I remember these graves are your homes now.

You are home forever.

And you will never go home again.

I touch the top of every tombstone.

I trace and retrace your chiseled names.

Each is as close to a hug as I can give you now.

My grandmother taught me not to step on graves.

Her ex-husband said, "the dead don't care."

I tiptoe between your plots.

I make sure my feet never trample on your bodies.

The grass is wet today, and I just noticed.

My shoes are getting damp.

If you walk in the fog long enough, you get soaked.

Your clothes get heavy with moisture.

I wonder what sticks to me here.

I take a moment and feel the air — it's still.

I close my eyes.

When I open them, you are all still dead.

And I am still alive.

X.

They call it survivor's guilt:
that aching feeling that I let you all down,
that I should have jumped in front of a bullet,
any bullet,
to save someone,
anyone.

It is the feeling that I should be buried
beside you — a twenty-seventh grave.

Sometimes,
on the memorial,
I search for my name,
knowing if I found it,
I'd claw back my nails
as I tried to crawl inside it.

Sometimes,
I imagine I'm ash.

Sometimes
I walk around for days
wondering if I'm a ghost
and you, beautiful youth, live on
as if you never knew me.

But Steven,
when I reach your grave
I feel relieved that it was you and not me.

You bully.

You beast.

How many times did I send you to the dean
for shoulder-checking someone in the hall,
for slamming a kid against a wall,
for dumping out a bookbag,
for saying "freak" or "fag,"
for projecting your hurt
where it didn't need to be.

Steven, I know,
I know I'm supposed to see
past your actions,
I'm supposed to punish the deed
and not the seed of such hurt…
but your confidence
and buoyancy,
the way coach never pulled you
from the game,
and how you'd smiled no matter what,
no matter the hurt you caused,
no matter the pain…

Steven,
you are so easy to hate.

Steven,
maybe in death
you will reflect,
look down on the football field
you loved so much in life,
knowing you are trapped on this hill —
detention forever,
eternity to fill,
with the likes of Kyle,
the coward,
too afraid to share,
too afraid to do anything
other than stare at his shoes,
and be grateful too,
of how he wasn't on your list to abuse.

Steven and Kyle —
a perfect pair!
One enables the other with silence,
compelling the first to violence.

XI.

Patti,
I saw you there among your friends,
a circle of hands held
around the flagpole,
praying.

Matthew and
Evan and
Rachel and
Stephanie and
Lisa —
I saw you there
each morning,
early,
together in prayer.

But for what did you pray?

Lisa: attention and fame,
your face plastered on
TV screens?
Maybe,
and if so,
dreams and prayers come true.
I wish you could speak now,
I wish I could ask you
how it feels to be an actress,
a Hollywood ghost
like Marilyn Monroe.

Stephanie: were your prayers,
like Lisa's,
answered in the wake
of bullets and blood and brains
splattered in the cafeteria
and the library and stairs?
I doubt it.
Your hands and mouth
may have been locked in prayer,
but your eyes read skeptic,
glazed with doubt —
apathetic.

Matthew: I see you asking God
for peace,
for strength,
for kindness.
And Matthew, I'm sorry,
but sometimes God
says no
even though
you've done
all the things
he's asked,
and you are left to grasp
for meaning in the dark,
the darkness of your grave.

Rachel: were your praying
for a place on Broadway?
If there is a heaven,
I hope you get to sing.
And if,
like we discussed
with Sartre and Camus,
this world is all there is,
know your voice plays,
until my death,
inside my ears.

Evan: so quiet,
so still,
afraid to talk in class,
I'm surprised you went out
and prayed with them.
Maybe you asked for a voice?
Maybe you asked for ears
to hear you?
I wish you
the strength to speak,
if ever again
the opportunity
may be seized.

Patti: leader of this ring,
what did you pray for
with all your Christian sincerity?
The souls of your peers?
The power to do God's will?
For safety,
forgiveness,
for strength to carry out
the great commission?
I ask you,
how successful,
how efficient,
were your prayers in stopping
the gunman's mission?

XII.

Patrick and John:

I can still see you
under the stairs,
the cards in your hands,
playing *Magic: The Gathering*.

You guys had your own life going.

Something different.

Something separate.

And still they gunned you down.

XIII.

Brian,
we are all hiding something,
we all have a closet.

But you,
Brian,
strong-willed boy in your
Joy Division tee,
purple fingernails,
and glittered cheeks —
you would have nothing
to do with hiding:
out and proud,
louder than your lesbian
counterparts,
you walked the halls
in your pride parade;
no wonder Mark was so afraid.

Brian,
When you took me aside
and started to cry,
confessing your love,
your kiss,
your relationship
with the letterman-jacket-jock,
I wasn't so much shocked
as I was stupefied.

Brian,
you reminded me
of my own time in
high school hell,
of my love for boys
that I was doomed to repel…
you were everything
I wished I could have been.

Brian,
you couldn't stand
the silence in which
Mark asked you to live,
you said
he made you feel
like you didn't exist
outside those hidden moments
when the two of you
would kiss,
and I wanted to tell you,
that kind of silence,
hot in your face
and cold in your chest,
was the silence
in which I have lived.

Brian,
I wanted to say,
"You know,
even the teachers
go to this school."
But this moment
was about you,
and the only advice
I could give
was that you get
one life to live —
it was a lame and cliché
thing for me to say,
but it was true
and no other words
would do.

XIV.

When I'm silent here,
and here is always silent,
save the sounds of cars passing on the highway,
I hear a chorus of your voices,
a Whitmatic catalog of song —
the varied carols of youth!
Each of you singing!
The whole world singing!

You sing
to keep vigil.
You sing
to remember.

Brian,
if for anyone I could
trade places,
I would trade places
with you.
I would give you this life,
let you keep living
a truth
I could never
live up to.

The sound of cries
and gunfire,
the hushed voices
of youth:
this is the hymn of the
American songbook.

I
hear
America
singing
through
bullets.

I
hear
America
singing
through
each
of
you.

About the Author

Dudgrick Bevins is a queer interdisciplinary artist from North Georgia who lives, teaches, and creates in New York City. His poetry volumes are published by bd-studios.com and Poet's Haven; he has also appeared in *Peregrine* and *Common Ground Review*, the micro-anthology *Queer, Rural, American* (University of Louisville Press), as well as various other online journals. He lives with his partner, the ghosts of two hedgehogs, and various other spirits who occasionally make themselves known. You can follow the artist and see a complete list of his publications and video work at www.dudgrickbevins.com.

Also published by bd-studios.com

Poetry Books

Georgia Dusk by Dudgrick Bevins & luke kurtis

Route 4, Box 358 by Dudgrick Bevins

Train to Providence by William Doreski & Rodger Kingston

Angkor Wat by luke kurtis

exam(i)nation by luke kurtis

the immeasurable fold by luke kurtis

(This Is Not A) Mixtape for the End of the World by Daniel M. Shapiro

Artists' Books

The Animal Book by Michael Harren

Tentative Armor by Michael Harren

Here Nor There by Sam Rosenthal

Just One More by Jonathan David Smyth

Architecture and Mortality by Donald Tarantino

The Male Nude by Michael Tice

Retrospective by Michael Tice